Sports Illustrated
SKIN DIVING
AND
SNORKELING

The Sports Illustrated Library

BOOKS ON TEAM SPORTS

Baseball   Football: Defense   Ice Hockey
Basketball   Football: Offense   Soccer
Curling: Techniques   Football: Quarterback Volleyball
  and Strategy

BOOKS ON INDIVIDUAL SPORTS

Badminton   Horseback Riding   Table Tennis
Fly Fishing   Judo   Tennis
Golf   Skiing   Track: Running Events
Handball   Squash

BOOKS ON WATER SPORTS

Powerboating   Small Boat Sailing
Skin Diving and Snorkeling   Swimming and Diving

SPECIAL BOOKS

Dog Training   Training with Weights
Safe Driving

Sports Illustrated

SKIN DIVING
AND
SNORKELING

By BARRY ALLEN

Illustrations by
Russ Hoover

J. B. LIPPINCOTT COMPANY
Philadelphia and New York

The author wishes to acknowledge the invaluable assistance of Ken Brock, Fred Calhoun, Dr. Betty Spears, Arthur Ullrich, Nancy Bates, Phil Holt, Dr. Reagh Wetmore and New England Divers.

U.S. Library of Congress Cataloging in Publication Data

Allen, Barry.
  Sports illustrated skin diving and snorkeling.

  (The Sports illustrated library)
  1. Skin diving. I. Title. II. Title: Skin diving and snorkeling.
GV840.S78A37 1973   796.2'3   72–14150
ISBN–0–397–00969–0
ISBN–0–397–00970–4 (pbk.)

Photographs on pages 10, 13, 14, 17, 18, 21, 22, 60, 77, 78, 80–81 and 86: Ron Church

Photographs on pages 47 and 84: Barry Allen

Cover photograph: Ron Church

Third Printing

Contents

Sports Illustrated
SKIN DIVING
AND
SNORKELING

1
The Sport

BENEATH THE SURFACE of the water lies another world. It is vast and relatively unexplored. Within it we are freed from gravity and can move through three dimensions. Experiencing this other world can be as uncomplicated as diving while holding your breath. This is skin diving.

Skin diving is an ancient profession. We know that pearls have been prized for thousands of years. Earliest historical records tell of battles lost or won because underwater soldiers were able to cut enemy anchor lines or neutralize submerged harbor defenses. Accounts of raising sunken treasure date from the time of Alexander the Great's reign (336–323 B.C.) and before. Pearling, underwater warfare and deep salvage were practiced for centuries by divers who relied mainly on their ability to hold their breath. Today in Japan, Korea and Polynesia there are still professional breath-hold divers who make their living harvesting animal and plant life from the sea.

As a sport, however, skin diving is not old. It began in the 1930's among a small group of adventurers on the Mediterranean coast of France. They went naked into the sea, gleefully stabbing fish. Since that time the popularity of skin diving has grown explosively. So has snorkeling, with surface air supplied to the snorkeler through a simple tube, and scuba diving, with compressed air carried by the diver on his back. The two largest scuba-diver training agencies in the United States now offer certified instruction in skin diving as well. (The word "scuba" is made up of the first letters of the words "self-contained underwater breathing apparatus.") Of the many people who practice both skin diving and scuba diving, some prefer skin diving because it means liberation from bulky equipment and provides an exhilarating physical challenge.

The skills of skin diving are absolutely basic to the enjoyment of underwater sports. Spearfishing and underwater photography are popular skin-diving activities. Thorough training in skin diving is essential preparation for a scuba-diving course. A scuba diver who runs out of compressed air is transformed into a skin diver. Then he must rely on his skill with mask, fins, snorkel and inflatable vest to return to shore and leave the water as healthy and happy as he entered it.

2
Where to Start

CERTIFIED INSTRUCTION

BEGIN SKIN-DIVER TRAINING under the guidance of
a professional, certified instructor. There are several na-
tionally organized groups in the United States that certify
diving instructors. At least two have set standards for training in skin diving. These are the National Association of
Underwater Instructors, abbreviated NAUI (National Headquarters: 22809 Barton Road, Colton, California, 92324),
and the National Board of YMCA's (National YMCA Scuba
Headquarters: 1611 Candler Building, Atlanta, Georgia,
30303). Assistance in locating certified instruction in skin
diving can be obtained through these two organizations.

Skin-diver training often begins in a swimming pool. In
regions where the requirements of warmth (about 80° F.)
and clarity are met in naturally occurring bodies of water,
where shallow, unobstructed areas can be isolated from the
open water and where adequate deck or beach space is
available for out-of-water instruction, you can safely and
effectively learn the basics of skin diving and snorkeling

outdoors. Perfect your skin-diver skills in confined water, whether in a pool or sheltered cove. Then you will be ready to move into open water, accompanied at first by your instructor. Learn well and enjoy it to the fullest extent.

PERSONAL FITNESS

Skin diving can be a strenuous physical activity. Have a physician give you a thorough physical examination before you begin training. Have his approval to participate in the sport, or leave it alone. Rapid and large changes in pressure characterize the diver's environment. It is essential that your body's ability to compensate for these changes (see Chapter 5) not be impaired by injury or disease. Your body should also be capable of adapting to the stress of cold-water immersion (see Chapter 8). Your doctor may be unfamiliar with the specific physical requirements of skin diving. Take a diving medical application form, which should be available through your instructor, to the examination.

3
Watermanship

WATER–SKILLS TEST

WATERMANSHIP is the ability to maintain oneself in the water safely and with justified confidence, even under adverse conditions. Good watermanship is a prerequisite for skin-diver training. Measure your own by taking the water-skills test described below. Perform all the skills without equipment.

(1) Demonstrate, to your instructor's satisfaction: the crawl kick (flutter kick) without using your hands, the side stroke and the breast stroke. The crawl kick will be the basis for swimming with fins. The side stroke will be needed in the rescue practice that is essential to any skin-diving course. The breast stroke is the preferred stroke for swimming underwater without fins.

(2) Swim a distance of at least 200 yards, using any stroke or combination of strokes. Your objective is to swim a continuous distance, so go slowly but do not stop to rest.

Later, in open water, your comfort and safety will depend more on endurance than speed.

(3) Tread water for 3 minutes or more (1 minute with your hands out of the water).

(4) Float on your back with a minimum of movement for 1 minute or more.

(5) Float face down while holding your breath. (Take only one deep breath beforehand.)

(6) Jump feet first into 8 feet of water. As you descend, equalize air pressure in your ears and sinuses with the surrounding water pressure by pinching your nose shut and gently exhaling against your closed nostrils.

(7) Swim underwater for at least 10 yards without a dive or a push-off.

(8) Dive into deep water head first, equalize as you descend and retrieve a 5-pound weight from a depth of 8 to 10 feet.

If you are able to perform these skills, you are ready to begin skin-diver training. If you have trouble with these skills, discuss this with your instructor. He will evaluate your ability in the water and advise you to proceed with skin-diver training or to work on your swimming first.

At the completion of skin-diver training, your watermanship will have improved further. You should be able to do the following:

(1) Tow a motionless swimmer about your size 50 yards.

(2) Swim underwater 25 yards.

(3) Swim 440 yards (a quarter mile) without stopping.

(4) Support yourself at the surface for 15 minutes using the "drownproofing" method described later in this book. (See page 64.)

Perform these skills in rapid succession, without a break, and in the order listed. This will require you to swim a good distance when tired, a situation you might confront under actual diving conditions. If you can bring your breathing back to its resting rate during the drownproofing exercise, you will have acquired an extremely valuable skill.

4
Basic Gear

THE MASK

ALTHOUGH THE HUMAN EYE has the ability to see extremely well in air, unaided vision is badly blurred underwater. You can remedy this situation by trapping air over your eyes with a diver's mask.

A mask covers your nose and eyes. Goggles, on the other hand, cover only your eyes. You have probably seen surface swimmers use goggles to protect their eyes from irritation. When you are diving, you must blow additional air through your nose into the trapped space as you descend so you can counteract the increase in water pressure outside. This maneuver is essential in preventing an injury called face squeeze (see page 46). It would, of course, be impossible to do this with goggles. A mask may have small, separate lenses for each eye, and would therefore resemble goggles. Closer inspection, however, would reveal that the nose is included in the air space, just as it is with the more familiar masks having one large lens.

23

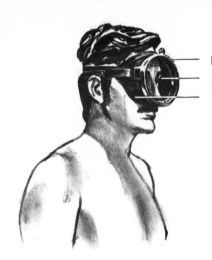

Band
Safety glass
Rubber skirt

Figure 1. Anatomy of the mask.

Mask Selection and Fit. Select a mask that is well made. The words "tempered," "shatterproof," "safety glass," or some similar phrase should appear on the lens as your assurance that it will not break easily. The possible danger to your eyes is obvious. The mask must also have a corrosion-resistant band which clamps the rigid lens or lenses in place within the flexible rubber skirt. (See Figure 1.) It is possible to buy an inexpensive mask with a plastic lens and no band. The plastic lens will fog hopelessly, become scratched and, with nothing to hold it in place, always be in danger of falling out.

There are masks which have one or a pair of built-in snorkels bristling from the top. The snorkels curve downward at their ends and are fitted with float valves. In air the floats fall, opening the snorkels to the atmosphere. Underwater, however, the floats rise, closing the tubes to prevent the mask from flooding. This, at least, is the theory. Each breath inhaled through the snorkels must first fill the mask itself before it can reach the diver's lungs. The last air to be exhaled remains in the mask, where it is first to be inhaled. Carbon dioxide (CO_2), the waste product of respiration, will accumulate in the relatively large volume

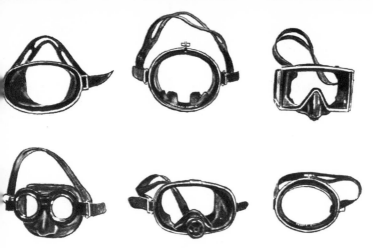

Figure 2. Mask types.

of the snorkel mask, possibly reaching dangerous levels and causing dizziness, nausea and eventual unconsciousness. Avoid this hazard by using a snorkel separate from the mask.

Masks come in many shapes and sizes to match the variety of human heads and faces. (See Figure 2.) Good fit keeps the water out. (See Figure 3.) Strapping a leaky mask more tightly to your head will not cause it to seal. Take time to find a comfortable, well-fitting mask.

Figure. 3. Hold a mask up to your face without using the headstrap. Position the mask for comfort, inhale slightly and take your hands away. If the mask falls, then it is not sealing.

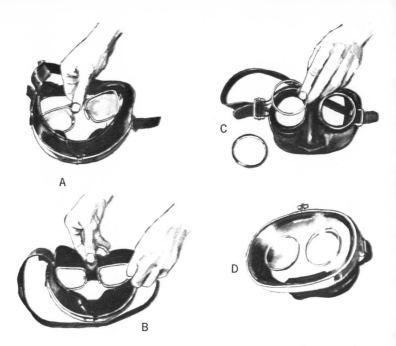

Figure 4. (A and B) You can sometimes wear ordinary eyeglasses under your mask if you remove the temple pieces from the frames and then tape the frames inside the mask. (C) Some opticians can grind special lenses to your prescription, which they will bond to the inner surface of your face plate. (D) Masks are also available which have separate, round lenses for each eye. These lenses can sometimes be removed, ground and then reinstalled.

Eyeglasses Underwater. If you normally rely on eyeglasses for good vision on land, your enjoyment of diving may be limited if you do not wear adequate corrective lenses underwater. Some methods for correcting your vision underwater are illustrated. (See Figure 4.) If you normally wear contact lenses, you may be tempted to try them under your mask. But if your mask were flooded or lost, you would have to shut your eyes to avoid losing the contact lenses. Ask your diving instructor and your ophthalmologist to help you select the best method of correcting your vision underwater.

Lens fogging can be a problem with any mask. It occurs when moisture in your breath condenses on the cold glass surface. This is less likely to occur if the glass is clean. Clean the inside surface of the lens by spitting on it and scrubbing the saliva with your fingers until they squeak on the glass. Then rinse the mask lightly. A mild, non-detergent soap, warm water and hard scrubbing may be needed to clean a particularly dirty or oily lens.

Even with clean glass, some fogging is unavoidable. If it occurs underwater, let a small amount of water into the mask, then look downward and move your head from side to side to wash the fog from the lens. When the lens is defogged, clear the water out of the mask, using the method to be described shortly.

Figure 5. There is a trick to putting the mask on: assure the face seal first, then pull the strap down over the back of your head. It may seem more natural to put the strap behind your head first and then drag the mask down over your face, but this will pull your hair down into the mask, causing a poor seal.

Putting Mask On. Practice fitting the mask to your face until you can do it smoothly and quickly. (See Figure 5.) Efficiency will be important later in mask exercises because you will be holding your breath while trying to complete them underwater.

Mask Clearing. The purpose of a mask is lost if it becomes flooded. If this happens at the surface, raise your head above the water and pull the bottom of the mask

Figure 6. Stand in waist-deep water. Hold your mask underwater and allow it to fill as you remain standing. Sit down, keeping your upper body vertical. Your partner should hold you under if necessary, releasing you instantly if you want to come up. Put the mask on underwater, press the top, tilt your head back about 45 degrees and exhale forcefully through your nose. If you are bothered by water going up your nose, start exhaling through it before you tilt your head. If you have difficulty blowing through your nose, exhale through your nose underwater without your mask. Practice until you can produce a steady stream of bubbles. If you do not tilt your head enough or if you tilt it too much, some water will be trapped in the mask. Pushing too hard on the top of the mask will cause the bottom to lift off your face and admit water.

away from your face to let the water drain. In deeper water, however, a quick ascent to the surface would be inconvenient. Try mask clearing underwater. (See Figures 6 and 7.)

There are masks which are fitted with purge valves, whose purpose is to let water out but not in; they can make mask clearing easier. When selecting a mask with a purge valve, look for one with a large valve opening, for it will facilitate clearing. Purge valves are shut by external pressure, but open readily if you exhale into the mask. The techniques of clearing already described for conventional masks change if you use a purge-valve mask. (See Figure 8.) If you intend to dive with a purge-valve mask, learn to clear a conventional one as well. This will allow you to use any mask.

28

Figure 7. To clear your mask while swimming horizontally, roll your body to one side until you are almost on your back. Press the side of your mask that is now uppermost and exhale through your nose. Be sure not to press the lowest side of your mask by mistake.

Figure 8. To clear a purge-valve mask, look downward as you exhale through your nose. Press the lens on either side of the purge with the fingers of one hand. The purge valve must be the lowest point of the mask.

THE FINS

Underwater swimming is unlike swimming at the surface. A complete surface-swimming stroke involves arms and legs. But a complete stroke is almost never used in skin diving, since the diver's hands should be kept free to handle equipment or to assist a diving partner. Fins are essential to the diver because the legs alone must be able to supply the power he needs.

Fin Selection and Fit. Fins must fit you well. If too tight, they will cause painful cramping; if too loose, they may chafe or fall off. When you progress to open water you may need to wear special insulated footwear. Select fins that will fit comfortably over the thermal protection you will need to wear in your local open-water conditions. (See page 89.) In warm water you will need the special boots or socks not for insulation but to assure a perfect fit and protect your feet from chafing.

Some fins have full foot pockets which cover the bottoms and sides of your feet. Other fins are open at the heel, having fixed or adjustable straps to hold them in place. (See Figure 9.) Full-foot fins may be the most comfortable design. Heel-strap fins, however, are probably the most se-

Figure 9.

Heel-strap fins.   Full-foot fins.

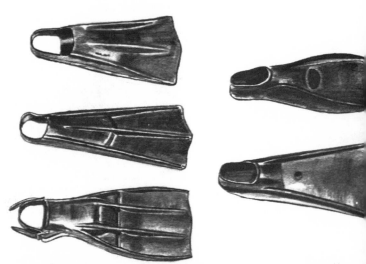

Blade kept
parallel to calf

Figure 10. Finning: blade position.

cure on your feet. For this reason the largest fins, with which a diver can generate a greater thrust, are usually equipped with heel straps. If you intend to buy fins with adjustable heel straps, make sure the buckles are sturdy and can be fastened securely.

Fins with long, stiff blades are impressive; so are the muscle cramps they will cause if you are not used to them. Small, flexible blades are best for your first season of diving. Fins work most efficiently when the blades are held roughly parallel to the lower leg. (See Figure 10.) If your fins are flat, you must point your toes, and this may be uncomfortable at first. Consider buying fins in which the blades are mounted at a downward angle to the foot pockets rather than in the same plane. (See Figure 11.) These fins will make it possible for you to keep the blades in the best position for swimming without having to point your toes completely.

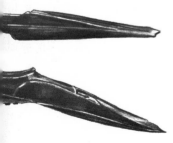

Figure 11. Flat fin and angled fin.

Putting Fins On. With fins, as with all other pieces of diving equipment, it is important to establish from the very beginning that you are master. Mastery of diving equipment begins with the basic act of putting it on. Learn to put your fins on efficiently. Avoid doing it in a way that requires you to hop around on one foot; sit down while putting them on. Wet your fins first so that they will slide easily over your feet. With your fins on securely, practice walking backward, not stepping but shuffling your feet. Practice this on the deck and then in shallow water. If you try to walk forward with fins, you risk a fall.

Figure 12. Swing your legs from your hips. Arch your back to keep your head high but your feet low. Keep your hands at your sides. Avoid letting your legs cross. Allow your knees to bend, but keep them still enough to transmit power from your hips down to your fins. An easy mistake is to flex your knees so that your feet move in circles as if you were peddling a bicycle, causing your thighs almost to push you backward.

Figure 13. Notice how much easier it is to fin on your back than on your stomach.

Finning. The flutter kick, which is normally used in the crawl stroke in surface swimming, is used by itself for swimming underwater with fins. Try this kick on your stomach and then on your back at the surface. (See Figures 12 and 13.)

A second leg stroke that is useful with fins is the dolphin kick. The legs are kept together as they are moved in an undulating motion. You may find this kick somewhat more difficult to learn than the flutter kick, but it can provide extremely effective propulsion. (See Figure 14.)

Fins put increased demands on leg and body muscles. When mastered, finning will seem as natural to you as swimming barefooted. Try all the exercises of the Water-Skills Test (page 19), including the 200-yard swim, using fins but not hands. Your ability to swim long, continuous distances will be important later.

A

B

C

34

Figure 14. The dolphin kick. (A) Straighten your legs and let them incline downward in the water as you bend slightly at the hips. (B) Start the kick by raising both legs together, still keeping them straight. (C) When your whole body is straight, continue moving your lower legs upward but move your upper legs downward, bending at the knees to make these opposing movements possible. (D) When your knees are flexed at a right angle, drive your lower legs down together until your legs are again straightened and inclined downward in the water. (E) Repeat the cycle.

D

E

THE SNORKEL

The snorkeler breathes surface air while his chest is surrounded by water at a greater pressure. The muscles of the diaphragm and chest wall must overcome the excess external pressure at each breath. At depths of more than just a few feet it would be as if your diving partner were standing on your chest as you tried to breathe. The longer the snorkel, the heavier the weight on your chest.

Selection and Use. Near the surface, however, the snorkeler is in his element. Snorkel breathing can be virtually effortless; it allows you to breathe while almost completely submerged, taking full advantage of the capacity of the water to support your body. Use a snorkel that is short; keep your chest high in the water and almost horizontal to minimize the water pressure surrounding it. (See Figure 15.)

Figure 15. Choose a snorkel that is a simple tube, one that is relatively short (12 to 14 inches) and bent in the shape of the letter "j." Avoid tubes with sharp bends, corrugations and small diameters. Minor reductions in flow may not seem important while breathing at rest, but heavy exertion can make air consumption increase thirtyfold.

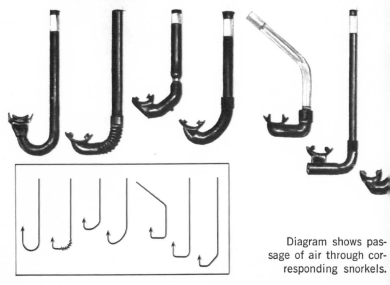

Diagram shows passage of air through corresponding snorkels.

Some snorkels have purge valves at the bottom, whose purpose is to let water out. A purge valve can work well on a mask because it is usually the only potential exit for water in the space. But it is poor logic to think that air and water can be driven through a purge valve at the lower end of a snorkel when it could leave freely through the open top. Some snorkels also have float valves at the top, whose purpose is to keep water out; these consist of a Ping-Pong ball held captive in a tiny cage. They often do not work when they are supposed to and are not under the diver's control.

Notice the construction of the snorkel's mouthpiece. The smaller part is the bitepiece. Clamp it between your teeth. The large oval lip flange, surrounding the bitepiece, fits between the outside of your teeth and the inside of your lips. Form a seal by pursing your lips around the flange. Biting harder will not improve the seal; it will only destroy the snorkel. If a leak persists, try another snorkel. Wear the snorkel on the left side of your head. If you take up scuba diving later, the snorkel will not interfere with the hose of most scuba regulators, which will lie next to the right side of your head.

Take your snorkel into the shallow water and practice snorkel breathing without a mask. (See Figure 16.) This is not impossible, just difficult at first. You can achieve control over your soft palate, a curtain of tissue at the back of

Figure 16. Seal the snorkel in your mouth and hold it in place with your left hand if necessary. Carefully submerge your face, including your nose, and breathe slowly through your mouth. If you do not inhale through your nose, no water will enter it.

your mouth that ordinarily closes your nasal cavities off from your throat when you swallow. This control will allow you to breathe through your snorkel without discomfort even if your mask is flooded or lost, an invaluable skill in emergencies.

Snorkel Clearing. When a snorkeler sees something beneath the surface that deserves a closer look, he holds his breath and dives (more about this on page 54), keeping his snorkel in his mouth. He does not need to plug the snorkel with his tongue. Water will invade the tube but will not enter his mouth unless he inhales. When he returns to the surface, he blows the snorkel clear and breathes through it once again. (See Figure 17.)

All the snorkel exercises described so far should be done without a mask. Mastery of them will make using a snorkel with a mask seem simple and natural, just as it should be.

Figure 17. Breathe through the snorkel a few times, then hold your breath and submerge. When you ascend, do not lift your face out of the water to breathe. Instead, blow into the snorkel as it just pokes above the surface. The water surrounding your chest adds its pressure to your efforts, increasing the force of your exhalation. Therefore, the deeper you are, the easier it will be to clear your breathing tube. Be sure that the tip of the snorkel is above the surface. You need only a simple puff, not a powerful blast.

THE INFLATABLE SAFETY VEST

If a skin diver becomes incapacitated for any reason, his mouth and nose must be kept out of the water. It is imperative to dive with a partner who is close enough to help. It would be difficult, however, even for a highly experienced person to keep an unconscious diver's face out of the water while towing him to safety. An inflatable safety vest is needed to keep the victim's head up.

Vest Selection and Use. When choosing an inflatable safety vest, select one made specifically for diving. Look for a vest equipped with a self-contained capsule of compressed gas to permit rapid inflation of the vest under power. Vests that achieve powered inflation through a hose connection to a scuba cylinder are, of course, of no use to a skin diver. Nor are they of any help to a scuba diver if his tank is empty. Vests that can be inflated only by mouth are useless to a diver incapacitated by fatigue, panic, cold or injury. Powered inflation by a compressed gas is an essential feature of a diver's safety vest. The compressed gas is generally either CO_2 contained in a one-shot cartridge or compressed air in a small, rechargeable cylinder. A CO_2 cartridge must be punctured to release its gas. Punctured cartridges are easily replaced. CO_2 cartridges are rated according to the weight of gas they contain. Cartridges which contain 8 grams, 12 grams, 16 grams or even 25 grams of compressed CO_2 are available. (There are 28.3 grams in an ounce.) These quantities do not include the weight of the steel cartridge.

The capacities of gas cylinders on compressed-air vests are given as the volume the air would occupy if released at sea level. This volume is usually measured in cubic feet or liters. (There are 28 liters in a cubic foot.)

One gram of CO_2 could potentially provide more than 1 pound of buoyancy when released into a vest near the surface. Therefore, a 25-gram cartridge could produce over

25 pounds of buoyancy near the surface. One cubic foot of air would provide more than 60 pounds of buoyancy under the same conditions. More of either gas would provide more buoyancy, until the vest was stretched to its maximum volume. Additional gas would escape through the pressure-relief valve or could rupture the vest if it had no such valve.

More gas is required to inflate a vest subjected to the pressure of increased depth than is needed to inflate that vest near the surface, where the surrounding pressure is much less. A gas supply which just fills a vest at the surface will provide only partial inflation—and therefore only partial buoyancy—at depth. A larger supply would provide full inflation somewhere below the surface. Compressed-air vests offer the advantage of a large supply of gas, capable of fully inflating a vest several times near the surface or at least once at greater depths, giving full buoyancy in each case. If you purchase a vest which can bring you up from depth, learn how to slow your ascent by venting gas from the vest. Master this in confined water before you attempt powered ascent in open water.

In addition to a system for powered inflation, your vest must be equipped with a tube to permit inflation by mouth. This tube is fitted with a mouthpiece that is closed with a valve. These valves are either push-to-open or pull-to-open. The pushing or pulling is often done with the teeth, but some vests have a thumb button. When the mouthpiece or button is released, a spring closes the valve. Valves which pull to open will also function as a pressure relief, opening automatically if the gas pressure in the vest becomes too great. Excess pressure could occur in a number of ways. If, for example, you fully inflated your vest by mouth and then actuated the power inflator, enough gas for a full inflation would be forced into a vest already stretched to capacity. If the extra gas were not vented, the vest could rupture.

You will often fill your vest by mouth to rest briefly at

the surface, later deflating it to dive. While you float, the lower part of the vest may be squeezed flat by the surrounding water pressure, which forces the air to the top of the vest and into the area behind your neck. If the oral tube attaches to the vest in the lower, flattened area, it would be difficult to suck out the trapped air. For this reason the tube should feed into the vest high on the collar.

Your safety vest can be rendered useless by a single puncture. Select a vest whose envelope is constructed of the heaviest material, and guard it from contact with sharp objects. The construction of the envelope must survive repeated exposure to salt water, sunlight and extremes of temperature. The best material for the purpose seems to be an impregnated synthetic fabric. The fittings and rigging of the vest must all be corrosion-resistant.

If your vest has a zipper up the front, keep it completely zipped up so that your head cannot slip easily out of the collar. Some vest straps are designed so that they can be unfastened quickly when necessary with one hand. This is a "quick release" and is always used when securing a weight belt to the skin diver's waist (see page 91). The virtue of a quick release is, of course, that it can be easily undone. However, the danger of using it with a vest is that it could come undone by accident and fail to keep your mouth and nose above water.

Vest Maintenance. Because your inflatable safety vest may be essential in an emergency, have a fixed routine for checking all its critical components just before every dive. Check the powered inflator, the oral inflator, the inflatable envelope and the rigging. (See Figure 18.) This is the only way you can be reasonably sure your vest will work when you need it.

Perform a further test, one you will not need to do as frequently. Wade into chest-deep water. If your vest has an exposed CO_2 cartridge, make sure that no part of it is touching your bare skin. Pull the lanyard or open the compressed-air valve. The vest should inflate rapidly. It should

A

B

C

Figure 18. (A) Examine the power inflator first. If yours is a CO_2 vest, unscrew the cartridge. Discard it if punctured. Look into the throat of the firing mechanism. As you work the firing lever, a pointed pin should move in and out, but it does not travel far. The cartridge must be screwed in well enough so that the pin can puncture it. Now tug sharply on the lanyard. The whole mechanism ultimately depends on a piece of string. Make sure that yours is not rotted. Put the lever back in the up position, insert an un-punctured cartridge and screw it down firmly. (B) Check the oral inflator. Familiarize yourself with the operation of the valve at the mouthpiece. Inflate the vest by mouth. (C) Fold your arms across your chest and squeeze the inflated vest as hard as you can. Any leak indicates a defective vest which must be replaced. If your vest has passed inspection so far, deflate it. Before you suck out the last bit of air, remove any loose powder the manufacturer may have put inside to prevent the sides of the envelope from sticking together. Inhaling powder can be harmful. Check the rigging of the vest: the straps, buckles and other fasteners.

roll you over onto your back if you are face down. It should support your face well out of the water so you can breathe. These are all "shoulds." Does your vest accomplish them? Notice that the rapidly escaping CO_2 has cooled the cartridge. Your skin might have been frostbitten had it been in direct contact with the cartridge. If the vest fails to inflate, examine both the cartridge and the firing mechanism to determine the cause of the failure. If the vest is defective, replace it before you proceed.

Do not hesitate to expend CO_2 cartridges or compressed air in confined and open-water practice with your vest. CO_2 forms a weak acid in combination with water. Therefore, do not inhale the gas from the vest after CO_2 inflation. Remove the punctured cartridge and rinse the detonator thoroughly in tap water. Protect your vest from deterioration. Rinse it in tap water after each pool or open-water use, dry it indoors in a cool place and lubricate all moving parts with nontoxic silicone oil.

5
Skin-Diver Skills

BREATH HOLDING

THE SKIN DIVER stops all visible breathing movements while submerged, but internal body processes continue. Body cells go on consuming oxygen from stores in the blood, and they continue to produce CO_2. When CO_2 in the body rises to a critical level, the diver experiences an involuntary urge to breathe. This breaking point for breath holding puts a strict time limit on skin diving.

Hyperventilation is an easy but dangerous way of extending this limit. It is rapid, forced breathing that flushes CO_2 out through the lungs faster than the body produces it. If you hold your breath immediately after hyperventilating, the level of carbon dioxide in your body will be below normal and will take longer to build up to the breaking point. Hyperventilation allows you to hold your breath longer, but it does not increase the body's supplies of oxygen to compensate sufficiently for the extended breath-holding time. You may lose consciousness from insufficient oxygen without warning before experiencing the urge to

45

breathe. Those who do hyperventilate before skin diving are probably unaware of the risks.

There are better ways to increase breath-holding time. The most effective method is to relax. Active muscle consumes much more oxygen than resting muscle, and produces a proportionately high amount of CO_2. Psychological stress also increases oxygen consumption and CO_2 production. Avoid situations that cause anxiety, and relax. Relaxation is the art of using only those muscles required for the job at hand, which in this case is to swim underwater. You consume less oxygen and produce less carbon dioxide when swimming in a calm, relaxed state. A small increase in your speed underwater requires an even greater increase in your output of muscular energy, reducing your breath-holding time even further. Relaxed, slow movement underwater is the safe key to long breath-hold dives.

HANDLING THE PRESSURE

Water is a heavy substance, roughly 800 times heavier than sea-level air, and exerts a pressure on your body that increases rapidly with depth. The increased water pressure surrounding your body raises internal body pressures, including that of the blood. This will have no harmful mechanical effects provided you can maintain an equal pressure inside the body's rigid or semirigid air spaces. These air spaces consist of natural body cavities and include the air chambers associated with the ears (middle ears) and the sinuses. An additional air space is the artificial body cavity created by your mask. If the air pressure in any of these spaces is not increased accordingly as you descend, the blood vessels and tissues lining that space will begin to swell. This diver's injury is called squeeze. Squeezes are prevented by raising pressures in body air spaces to equal the external water pressure. This is called equalization. Plugs in the outer ear canals (the visible exterior openings

46

of your ears) cannot prevent the swelling of tissues and vessels lining the middle ear because that swelling results from increased pressure on the entire body. In fact, ear plugs are dangerous for diving. Water pressure drives them deep into the outer ear canals, thus isolating an area that is normally open to the water. A new body cavity is created, one that is completely sealed off and for which there is no possibility of equalization. A squeeze occurs between the eardrum and the plug.

Pressure equalization between the various spaces of the ears is easy to accomplish. On land, pinch your nose shut and try to blow gently through it. You should feel a sensation in both ears. You have forced air into your middle ear spaces through tubes (the Eustachian tubes) that connect these spaces with the back of your throat. You have probably forced air into your sinus cavities as well. Try this underwater while wearing a mask. (See Figure 19.) You may not be able to equalize if you have a head cold or sinus congestion. This is a strong reason for not diving until such a condition has cleared up.

You can equalize more easily with certain masks, especially those which have finger wells on either side of your nose. Be sure that you can equalize with your own mask in shallow water before you proceed. Never descend if you

Figure 19. To equalize the pressure in your ears, push the bottom of the mask up against your nostrils to close them, without disturbing the mask's seal on your face. Blow gently against your closed nostrils to force additional air into your middle ears.

cannot prevent even a mild discomfort in your ears. A squeeze can cause permanent injury. Begin equalizing the moment you submerge, and continue throughout the first 10 feet or so of your descent. You can equalize less frequently after that. If you wait until you feel discomfort, a squeeze will have begun. The tissues lining the affected space will have started to swell, reducing the diameter of the Eustachian tubes. Ascend to a point at which the swelling subsides enough to reopen the tubes, permitting you to equalize. If the squeeze is severe, this will not reduce the swelling. The tissues will need time to reabsorb fluids released into them. Therefore, start equalizing before any symptoms of squeeze can occur. If you have trouble getting air into your middle ears, clench your jaw or make a yawning motion as you blow to open your Eustachian tubes. The additional air you blow into your middle ears on descent must be vented on ascent. This often happens automatically. But if you experience discomfort in your ears on the way up, again clench your teeth or yawn to facilitate the outward passage of air.

The lungs and digestive tract are normally not subject to diver's squeeze. They are flexible and, unlike the rigid or semirigid spaces discussed so far, will be compressed as freely as rubber balloons, automatically adjusting the pressure of the gases they contain to equal the water pressure outside. After each exhalation the lungs do not collapse, but are held to the minimum volume to which the chest wall can contract: the residual volume.

As a breath-hold diver, you will find that increased water pressure will compress your chest, which will in turn raise the pressure of the air in your lungs. Your lung volume contracts in a way that resembles exhaling, except that no air escapes. If, for example, you descend 33 feet in the sea (34 feet in fresh water), the pressure on your body is double that which you experience at the surface, the pressure in the lungs is doubled to match and your lung volume will be compressed to approximately half. At 66 feet, the pressure on you is tripled, as is the pressure in your lungs, and your lung volume is reduced to one third, and so forth. If you descend far enough, your ever-decreasing lung volume will shrink to the residual volume. It was thought that if a diver were to continue his descent beyond this point, the air pressure in his lungs could not increase further even though the external water pressure would continue to increase. This sounds distressingly like the conditions that lead to a squeeze. It has been observed recently, however, that something else does take place in this situation. The blood vessels within the lungs are extremely elastic. Blood is directed to them from other parts of the body, causing them to swell without injury, reducing the volume of the lungs. Thus, as you go beyond the depth at which your chest wall can continue to contract, the very elastic blood vessels in your lungs take over the task of pressure adjustment. There are limits beyond which human breath-hold divers dare not descend. Time places the strictest of all limits on skin-diving depth. Blackout from insufficient oxygen is perhaps the skin diver's greatest peril. Always allow extra time for ascent. Never descend beyond half the distance you can swim horizontally underwater near the surface.

We mentioned another critical body air space, the cavity contained within the mask. This space qualifies as a body cavity because one of its walls is your face. As you descend, blow into the mask to equalize the air pressure in this cavity with the increase in external water pressure. This will prevent swelling of facial blood vessels. (See Figure 20.) The victim of a mask squeeze will have two spectacular black eyes.

Figure 20. To equalize the pressure in your mask, blow into it through your nose. Exhale into your mask frequently on descent until a few bubbles escape under the mask skirt into the water, indicating that air pressure inside the mask exceeds the water pressure. Bubbles will continue to escape until the air pressure inside the mask equals the pressure outside, which is exactly what you want.

ENTRIES

When you enter the water, your first objective is to establish a safe, stable position on the surface. In such a position you can make final adjustments of equipment, reestablish contact with diving partners and take an exploratory look below. All this is normally done before a descent is attempted. A proper entry puts you in the water easily but stops you at the surface. The type you use depends on the situation. The best entry off a gently sloping beach in calm conditions will be a backward shuffle into chest-deep water. Off a rocky shore it may be best to climb down into the water.

In no case should you dive head first while wearing skin-diving gear. If you do, your mask and snorkel will come slamming into your face. At deep water, off a pier or a boat, a jumping or falling entry may be best. The most useful of these is the stride entry. It may be used in any situation where a level platform is adjacent to deep, unobstructed water. A dock, flat rock, breakwater or large, stable boat with a low gunwale may all be good places to use this entry. Check the depth at your intended point of entry to be sure you will not hit bottom. In cloudy water, a pole or weighted line will tell the depth. Before you leap in, make sure there is also an easy exit. If your entry platform is too high and its sides are slippery, you may have trouble pulling yourself out. Find a lower entry point or get a ladder. Practice the stride entry at the edge of deep, unobstructed water in full skin-diving gear. (See Figure 21.)

If you have the good fortune to be diving off a boat, you may be prevented from using the giant-stride entry by a gunwale or railing that reaches waist level. In this case, do a back entry. (See Figure 22.) Practice this entry in full skin-diving gear at deep water.

Figure 21. For the stride entry, hold your mask in position by pressing the fingers of one hand firmly on the lens. Spread your fingers so you can see out. Cup the bend in your snorkel with the palm of the same hand. Stride out over the water as if it were solid ground. Kick your legs together just as your ankles are starting to get wet and, as you sink lower, force your arms down through the water to your waist. Your kick and arm motion will bring you to a halt, with just your head above the surface.

Figure 22. For the back entry, sit on the edge, tuck your head to your chest, hold your mask and snorkel and fall backward, hitting the water with your shoulder blades.

A   B

SURFACE DIVES

Once in the water and ready to go below, perform a surface dive. Raise part of your body (head or legs) above the surface, where it will no longer be buoyed up by the water. Allow yourself to sink. When your head is about one body length underwater, begin finning downward. Exhaling a small amount of air on the way will decrease your buoyancy, making the descent almost effortless, reducing exertion that otherwise would cut down on your breath-holding time.

There are three types of surface dives. Each relies on the principles outlined above. The simplest of the three is the feet-first surface dive; it is particularly useful whenever water visibility is poor or bottom conditions unknown. (See Figure 23.)

Figure 23. (A) Start the feet-first sur-face dive by treading water. Press your arms down to your sides and kick your legs together. (B) Keep your legs together and your arms at your sides as you rise smoothly. The weight of your upper body out of the water will start to pull you down. (C) As your shoulders submerge, sweep your arms upward to push yourself still lower. (D) When you are submerged about one body length, pull your knees to your chest and lower your head. As your head goes down, your body will rotate. (E) When you uncoil from this position, you should be horizontal and ready to swim underwater.

C

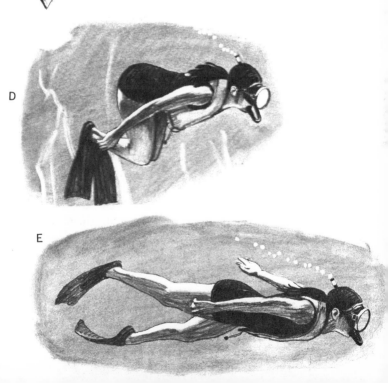

D

E

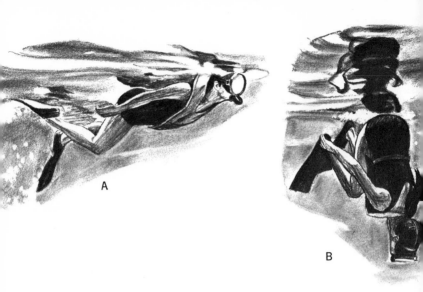

A

B

Figure 24. (A) Keep finning as you go into the tuck surface dive. (B) Bend at the hips and pull your knees and arms to your chest. (C) Thrust your legs straight up. Point your toes. Maintain this streamlined position and glide smoothly down. (D) To level off, arch your back. (E) Start finning.

There are times, however, when you will want to make a surface dive directly from a horizontal position while snorkeling. You will have two choices: the tuck or the pike. In both it is important to start with good forward momentum. The pike may be more difficult to do while wearing heavy fins because you must lift them while they are at the full length of your straightened legs. When you have mastered both horizontal surface dives, you can choose between them. (See Figures 24 and 25.)

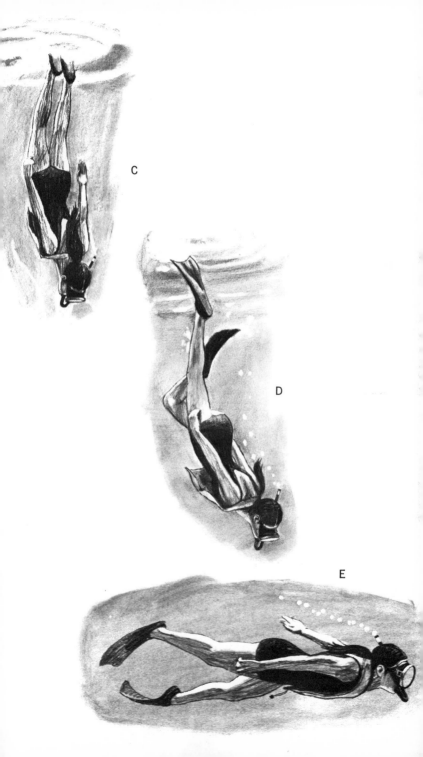

C

D

E

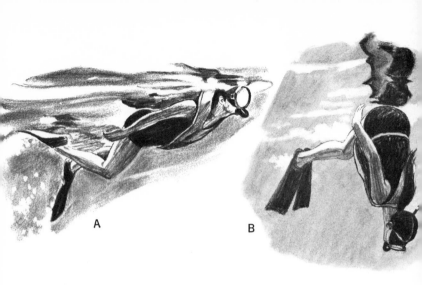

A

B

Figure 25. (A) Keep finning as you go into the pike surface dive. (B) Bend at the hips with your head down. Keep your legs straight and parallel to the surface. (C) Raise your legs straight up. Point your toes. Glide smoothly downward. (D and E) Complete the dive as you would the tuck.

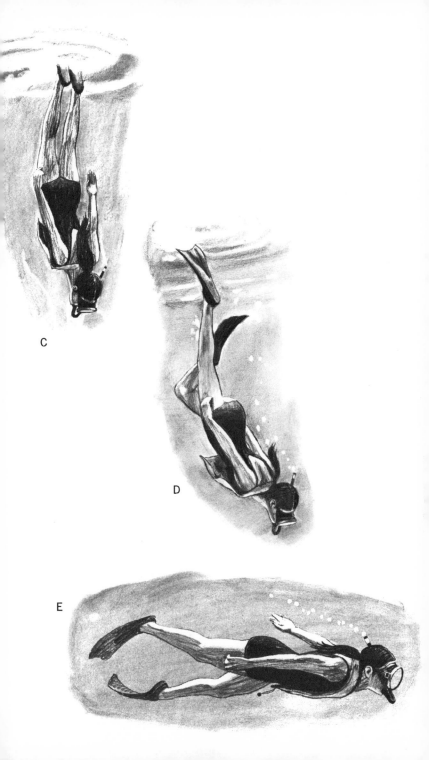

C

D

E

Figure 26. As you ascend, look up, extend one hand over your head and turn slowly. This will allow you to see where you are going and will protect your head should you be unable to avoid surfacing under an obstacle. Lower your extended arm before it breaks the surface. Waving an arm above the surface should be used only as a call for help.

ASCENTS

You must start an ascent well before you first feel the urge to breathe. (A scuba diver can inflate his lungs to full size at any depth. If he were to hold his breath and ascend as a skin diver would, his already full lungs would overexpand, causing grave injury. Any diver who takes a breath underwater must then breathe normally or exhale on the way up, something an ordinary skin diver is not required to do.) As you ascend, the water pressure around you decreases, the pressure of your lung gases—including oxygen —is reduced as well and your lungs expand again, reaching normal size at the surface. But it is precisely the pressure of these vital gases that drives them through lung membranes into the blood, where they can be utilized by the body. If you struggle to the surface, you need more oxygen because you are working harder but your supply is diminishing. Under these conditions, it is quite possible to lose consciousness on the way up. Start your ascent sooner, while you still carry a reasonable supply of oxygen in your blood, and make a more efficient, slow ascent. (See Figure 26.)

6
Surface Skills

UNDER THE SURFACE the downward force of gravity is neutralized by the buoyancy of your body in water, and you can hover effortlessly. But much of your time will be spent swimming or floating at the surface, where you will feel gravity's burden. If you are exhausted on returning to the surface, you may find that you cannot draw enough air through the snorkel. You will then have to dispense with it and raise your head to breathe. If you tread water to accomplish this, you will become even more exhausted and may soon be in serious trouble. This is an unbeatable argument for acquiring a high level of surface watermanship and for wearing an inflatable life jacket.

Surface skills have two objectives: (1) To meet effectively the challenge of a difficult situation, using your own resources and equipment. This is self-rescue. (2) To rescue another diver who can no longer help himself, apply any needed first aid and get the victim to a point of safety out of the water.

Not everyone can float on his back, but most can float

when face down in the water, provided the lungs contain a full breath. The body is most stable in this position when it is almost completely submerged, with just the top of the head and the shoulder blades awash. The ability to float with part of the body above the surface is called positive buoyancy. Those who cannot float at all have negative buoyancy. If, while floating, you raise a hand or arm out of the water, your body will sink until most of it is re-submerged and equilibrium is again achieved.

If you wish to keep part of your body out of the water, resisting this natural tendency to sink, you will have to work hard to do it. How hard? Your head may weigh 5 to 10 pounds. In treading water, you will have to supply the power to hold this weight out of the water.

SNORKEL FLOATING

A snorkel allows you to float face down yet breathe surface air. This is snorkel floating. (See Figure 27.) It can be done with or without a mask and is an invaluable skill for self-rescue. The snorkel has doubtless saved the lives of many divers who were too exhausted to tread water. Just as important, it has helped others conserve their energy, avoiding dangerous exhaustion. The snorkel is an essential piece of equipment, one you should carry on every dive. It is also an important convenience that permits you to look beneath the surface without having to lift your head for each breath.

VEST FLOATING

Practice handling your vest under less than ideal conditions while still training in confined water. This will help you prepare for open water. Inflate your vest orally while treading water. (See Figure 28.)

Figure 27. Snorkel floating.

Figure 28. Inflate the vest in rhythm with your breathing. Take a few smaller breaths between inflations if you start to feel breathless or dizzy. You should be able to achieve safe support with two or three normal exhalations and be able to inflate your vest orally even when slightly winded.

DROWNPROOFING

The snorkel and inflatable life jacket are essential equipment for surface survival, but as long as the diver is conscious, he should not depend totally on his equipment. Even the best maintained equipment can fail at a decisive moment. Drownproofing is a skill which will permit an exhausted skin diver to rest and breathe at the surface with no help from his equipment. It was developed by Fred Lanoue, Swimming Coach at Georgia Institute of Technology. (See his book, *Drownproofing*, published by Prentice-Hall, Englewood Cliffs, New Jersey, in 1963.) If a skin diver were not totally incapacitated, he could always rescue himself using this method, even if his equipment were to fail or be lost.

Figure 29. (A) If you are a good floater, start drownproofing vertically with your face submerged. Let your arms and legs hang down limply in the water. This is your resting position. (B) Get ready to take a breath. Slowly raise your arms at your sides to just under the surface and spread your legs in preparation to kick. (C) When you want a breath, bring your arms down and kick. These motions

A

B

There are three basic drownproofing techniques. One is intended for good floaters, one for marginal floaters and one for nonfloaters. The essential difference among the techniques is the angle of the drownproofer's body. If a person hangs vertically in the water, his chest will be deeper than if he were floating horizontally. Because water pressure increases with depth, the chest of the vertical floater will be compressed more, causing him some loss of buoyancy. Good floaters (women, children and some men) can float vertically. Poor floaters, who have no buoyancy to spare, will have to assume an almost horizontal position. Nonfloaters will have to be as horizontal as possible and must keep moving as well. Determine the category to which you belong by trying, with a full breath, the floating positions described above. Then practice the drownproofing exercises described below. (See Figures 29, 30 and 31.)

need not be forceful. Just before your mouth breaks the surface, exhale to make room for a comfortable breath. Rise above the surface no higher than your chin. Inhale through your mouth. (D) Fall to your resting position. If you cannot sink, you took too large a breath. With practice your resting times will increase to 10 seconds or more. Repeat the cycle.

C   D

A

B

Figure 30. (A) If you are a marginal floater, start drownproofing with your back at a 45-degree angle to the surface. Let your arms and legs hang down limply. Your head should be horizontal, with just the back of it above water. This is your resting position. (B) Get ready to breathe. Extend your arms out in front of you; cross your wrists with your palms facing out. Open your legs to prepare to kick. (C) When you want a breath, raise your head and start to exhale. Finish exhaling as your chin reaches the surface. (D) Stay up a little longer by sweeping your hands outward and down to your sides. Kick lightly. Inhale through your mouth. (E) Put your face in the water and assume the resting position again. Repeat the cycle. Your resting time can be increased to 10 seconds or so as you master drownproofing.

C

D

E

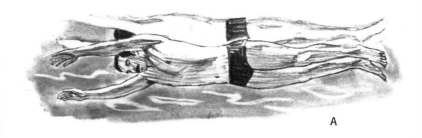

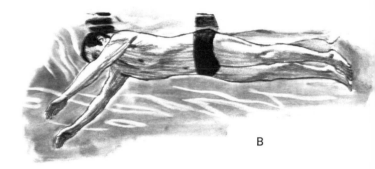

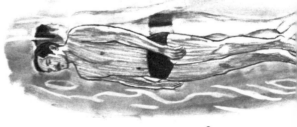

A

B

C

Figure 31. (A) If you are a nonfloater, start drownproofing by stretching out horizontally and extending your arms over your head. (B) Sweep your arms sideward and downward to your hips to keep moving forward and upward. (C) Glide. (D) As you near the surface, allow your legs to drop, but no more than 45 degrees. Open your legs in preparation to kick. Raise your arms to just under the surface and cross your wrists, with your palms facing outward. (E) Raise your head as you kick and sweep your arms outward and downward. Exhale quickly. When your mouth is above the surface, take as large a breath as possible. Put your face in the water. Extend your arms over your head, kick and glide. Repeat the cycle. As a nonfloater, you have no resting position. You must continually move forward. Complete the full stroke cycle every 3 seconds.

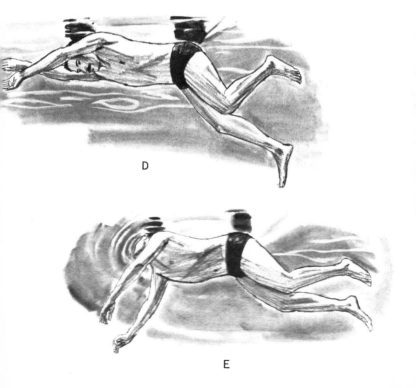

D

E

When you have achieved fair success with the method of drownproofing that best suits your own buoyancy, then practice it while removing and replacing your fins; while removing, replacing and clearing your mask; and while orally inflating your vest. Avoid treading water. Practice until you can perform these maneuvers without interrupting your downproofing rhythm.

RESCUE TECHNIQUES

There may come a time when you will be required to aid or completely rescue another diver. Panic, extreme exhaustion, cold exposure, serious injury or unconsciousness may make this necessary. If the hurt diver is underwater, bring him to the surface immediately, inflating his vest on the way up if possible. An inflated vest may not lift the victim to the surface, but it will help to support him once he arrives there. A victim who is already at the surface, or one who has been brought up, should be taken immediately to safety using an appropriate tow. (See Figures 32, 33 and 34.) Take extreme care that the victim's nose and mouth are kept out of the water.

Once you have achieved familiarity with your own vest and feel reasonably comfortable while operating it in the variety of situations mentioned above, then work with a partner. Each of you should start by inflating your own vest orally. Practice towing each other while wearing inflated vests.

The venerable but still excellent cross-chest carry—as taught by the American Red Cross—is ideal for rescuing swimmers, but it is difficult to use on divers wearing an inflated vest. In some cases you can slide your arm underneath the inflated vest and apply this carry as it is intended to be used. But this may be impossible if you are wearing a wet suit and have a depth gauge, compass or underwater watch strapped to your wrist.

70

Figure 32. You can tow your partner and achieve the best control of his head position by holding his head firmly between your palms while you kick on your back.

Figure 33. Tow your partner by the collar of his vest. Look to make sure his face is always well clear of the water. Remove his mask and snorkel to give him more air. Perform a side stroke with your free arm and a side-stroke kick (scissors kick) with your legs. Support your partner's lower body with your hip. Do not use this carry if it causes your partner's vest to press uncomfortably on his throat.

Figure 34. Try pushing your partner. Swim on your stomach while she places her hands on your shoulders, keeping her arms rigid. She is, of course, still on her back. You cannot control the position of your partner's head. Therefore, in an emergency situation, this method should only be used when a victim is still capable of keeping his own head up and his arms straight.

If in an emergency situation a distressed diver cannot inflate his own vest orally, he may be dangerously close to panic. Approach him underwater, from behind. Reach around him to pull the lanyard, inflating his vest under power. This maneuver requires familiarity with your partner's vest as well as your own. Learn the location of the lanyard on his vest and its proper operation. Practice this maneuver in confined water.

IN-WATER FIRST AID

The initial step in first aid for a diving injury is to tow the injured diver to a point where he can be removed from the water. The only exception to this occurs when the shore or a boat is more than a few seconds away and the victim is not breathing or is bleeding severely. Then, start first aid in the water. Death or irreversible damage could occur within minutes. Hemorrhage can be stopped or controlled by applying direct pressure over the wound with your hand. Artificial respiration can be performed successfully in the water. (See Figure 35.)

Of course, it is always more convenient to administer first aid on dry land. But you may have no choice: if the victim is to have any chance of survival, you must control serious bleeding immediately and begin artificial respiration within 3 minutes after his breathing has stopped. If the victim was submerged when recovered, you may have no accurate idea of how long he has not been breathing. Assume the worst. Begin artificial respiration immediately.

After the victim has been brought ashore or aboard a boat, send for medical help. Keep the victim quiet and on his back until a careful examination has ruled out serious injury, especially to the neck or back. Use extreme care in handling him. Splint obvious fractures of the limbs. Give nothing by mouth if the victim has an abdominal injury or is unconscious. Wrap blankets around him to maintain body warmth, but do not overheat.

Look for wounds, pain, tenderness, unusual shape or position of a body part and loss of function. Look for signs of concealed injury by checking the victim's general state of consciousness, breathing, pulse, strength, skin color and skin temperature.

Treat cold exposure immediately. People who have been chilled sufficiently to cause confusion or unconsciousness

Figure 35. To give in-water artificial respiration, inflate your own and the victim's vest. Float at a right angle to the victim; lean over him to make contact without getting on top of him. Check his mouth for obstructions and pull his head back to assure an open airway. Cradle his head in the crook of your elbow. Pinch his nose shut. Take a deep breath, seal your lips to his and exhale to inflate his lungs. Turn your face away from his. Take a breath as you keep an ear above his mouth to listen for his exhalation. Repeat 12 times a minute (every 5 seconds). If you and the victim are alone, make your way to safety without interrupting artificial respiration.

may not recover unless rewarming is started quickly. Remove wet equipment and wrap the victim in blankets or a sleeping bag. Allow him to rewarm from his own body-heat production. In severe cases of cold exposure, the victim's own body produces too little heat, and external heat will have to be applied. A hot bath, as hot as can be tolerated by hand, is the treatment of choice, but this is not available at most dive sites. The alternative would be for a warm, dry person to strip down and climb under the covers, rewarming the victim actively with his body heat.

The U.S. Coast Guard maintains a Search and Rescue Service that can reach most water locations quickly and can provide fast transport of the victim to a hospital. Police and fire-department rescue squads can also be called for assistance. As a diver, make it your business to know the availability of emergency services in your diving area. Keep a list of emergency phone numbers.

7
Putting It All Together

SO FAR, the skills of skin diving have been described as separate exercises, using one piece of equipment and performing one maneuver at a time. It is now important to begin putting these skills together in sequence while still training in confined water. This practice will increase your mastery of equipment and help you build patterns of skill needed in open-water situations. Here are seven practice sequences, each requiring different levels of ability. Eventually you should be able to do all of them.

(1) Jump feet first into water 8 to 10 feet deep, without fins or snorkel. Hold your mask in one hand, ready to put on. Equalize as you drop to the bottom, exhaling a little air to stay there. Put on your mask and clear it. Ascend, looking up, pointing up and turning.

(2) Follow instructions for number (1), above, but hold the snorkel with the mask. Fit the mask and snorkel on the bottom. Stay there to clear the mask. Ascend, looking up, pointing up and turning. Clear the snorkel as it just breaks the surface, then snorkel 10 yards without lifting your face out of the water.

79

(3) Follow instructions for number (2), above, but hold your fins under one arm as you drop to the bottom with your mask and snorkel in one hand. Keep the other hand free for pinching your nose to equalize. Fit the mask and clear it. Fit the snorkel and fins. Ascend, looking up, pointing up and turning. Clear the snorkel as it just breaks the surface, then snorkel 10 yards without lifting your face out of the water.

(4) Place a weight belt and 5 loose weights in a pile on the bottom, in 8 to 10 feet of water. Make an entry in full skin-diving gear. Perform a surface dive. Equalizing, descend to the weights. On the bottom, thread as many weights on the belt as you can. Ascend, looking up, pointing up and turning. Snorkel-float at the surface to rest while your partner descends to unthread the weights. Practice this over several water sessions until you can each thread or unthread all 5 weights at a time. Then try the exercise while wearing wet-suit gloves or heavy cloth work gloves.

(5) Make an entry with full skin-diving gear. Snorkel a short distance. Make a surface dive. Equalize as you descend to the bottom in 8 to 10 feet of water. Remove your mask completely. Replace and clear it while still on the bottom. Ascend, looking up, pointing up and turning. Clear your snorkel as it just breaks the surface. Snorkel-float as your partner tries this exercise. Repeat as needed.

(6) Use lead weights to mark two stations about 10 yards apart on the bottom in 8 to 10 feet of water. Wear full skin-diving gear and make an entry with your partner. Surface-dive and equalize as you each descend to one of the bottom stations. Once there, remove your mask, place it beside the marker and keep your eyes open as you exchange positions with your partner. Fit his mask to your face, clear it and ascend as usual. Snorkel-float to rest, then repeat.

(7) Cover the lens of your mask with aluminum foil, blacking it out completely. Have your partner watch you from the deck as you make an entry in full skin-diving

gear, wearing your blacked-out mask and a weight belt with a quick release. (See page 91.) Stay at the surface. Drop the weight belt with one hand; inflate your safety vest fully by mouth. Then deflate it completely. Remove your mask and climb out of the water. Watch your partner as he tries this exercise.

8
Open-Water Skin Diving

DIVING IN OPEN WATER is the reason and reward for skin-diver training. Confined water is a relatively controlled environment. The open water is not. Make your first open-water dives with your instructor. After these beginning dives, and when he feels you are ready, you will be awarded full skin-diver certification. Your training has not stopped at this point, but the responsibility for continuing it has been shifted from your instructor's shoulders and placed squarely on your own.

COLD WATER

Northern waters can provide as great a variety of diving experiences as southern ones, but an unprotected diver or swimmer has a poor chance of survival in water at 60° F. after only two hours' exposure. This is roughly the summer

temperature of the waters from Boston to the north on the Atlantic Coast, and from San Francisco to the north on the Pacific Coast. Temperatures of more southern waters will also fall to 60° F., or below, outside of the summer months. Some sort of exposure protection is required for diving in these waters.

Cold immersion puts a dangerous strain on individuals with heart disease or high blood pressure. People with such conditions should never deliberately expose themselves to cold water. Even in healthy individuals, cold immersion initially causes an involuntary increase in the rate and depth of breathing. In tests, individuals were asked to hold their breath 10 seconds after entering water at 40° F. They could not; they were unable to control their breathing for the first few minutes of their immersion. If a cold-water dive is planned, you should let your body adjust to partial immersion first; submerge your face only after you are sure you can hold your breath. This means that drownproofing must not be attempted at the beginning of cold immersion. The safety vest is important in this situation.

The initial reaction to cold immersion becomes less pronounced with repeated exposure. If you intend to dive in cold water, begin in the warm-water season and continue at frequent intervals as the water gets colder. Your body will then become accustomed to cold water. Infrequent diving in cold water is a dangerous practice.

Some people are allergic to cold. The skin becomes hot, red and blistered. The symptoms usually start only after the end of exposure. People with this problem should consult a doctor and should not dive in cold water without his approval.

COLD–EXPOSURE SUITS

Anyone who intends to dive in waters colder than 70° F. will need to wear an exposure suit. There are two general types: dry suits, whose insulation is provided by under-garments, and wet suits, which are made of an insulating material.

Dry suits trap air next to the diver's body and are generally constructed of thin rubber sheeting or of a rubber-impregnated fabric. The effectiveness of a dry suit depends on its watertightness. Any leak will soak the underwear, virtually eliminating its value as insulation.

The wet suit has revolutionized skin and scuba diving. It allows the diver to enter waters that would normally be forbiddingly cold and to submerge without the inconvenience of having to keep the suit watertight. Military divers have submerged in the waters of the Arctic and Antarctic wearing the standard ¼-inch wet suits. It must be added, however, that these military divers were well-conditioned to cold water.

Wet suits are so called because they normally allow a small amount of water to enter. They are constructed of a flexible foam (usually neoprene, a synthetic rubber) that is thicker than dry-suit material. The insulation value of the foam derives from the voids provided by the bubbles of gas trapped within the material. Any water that enters the suit is retained next to the skin, where it is insulated by the foam neoprene from the cold water outside and is quickly heated by the body to skin temperature. It then does not cause the diver further discomfort or undue heat loss. Wet suits provide varying amounts of thermal protection depending on their thickness; ⅛-, 3/16-, ¼- and 5/16-inch thicknesses are available. The 3/16- and ¼-inch thicknesses are the most common for full suits. A full wet suit consists of a long-sleeved jacket, long pants, separate boots, gloves or mitts and a hood (see Figure 36). One-eighth-inch material is often used for sleeveless shirts or for suits with short sleeves and legs. These partial suits may be worn alone in water above 70° F., but they may also be worn under a full suit to give added protection in unusually cold water.

Figure 36. Wet-suit hoods are available in all standard thicknesses. The best design has a large, attached skirt which can be tucked under the collar of a wet-suit jacket, effectively keeping cold water away from your neck. Hand protection can be provided by five-fingered gloves or by mitts, each constructed of wet-suit material. Gloves permit the use of all fingers, but mitts are warmer. Wet-suit foot protection consists of foam rubber socks or boots. Boots have a hard rubber sole for walking on rocks or other rough terrain above water. Be sure there is a layer of insulating foam between the hard sole and your foot. The hard rubber by itself is a poor insulator.

The parts of an exposure suit which cover your feet, head and hands are often referred to as accessories. They are definitely not accessories in waters colder than 60° F.

Wet suits are closed with zippers, usually at the chest, wrists and ankles. Suits for ladies are, of course, shaped differently and often have an additional zipper at one hip. Wet-suit zippers need not be watertight but must be of a noncorroding material.

Plain neoprene foam has little resistance to tearing; it tends to adhere to the body, making dressing difficult. This can be remedied by bonding a nylon fabric to the foam, reinforcing it and providing a slick lining that makes putting it on much easier. The inside surfaces of unlined wet suits can be lubricated with water or a sprinkling of talcum powder for easy entry. Make sure that the talcum powder you use on your suit is pure talc (magnesium silicate). Powder containing scent or oils will damage your suit. You can buy pure talc at a dive shop.

Waters above 70° F. may require no exposure suit at all. However, if you are thin, or if you are of average build but plan a long immersion, consider wearing a ⅛-inch foam shirt or short suit, or even a standard jacket (⅜-inch or ¼-inch). This will delay chilling and make your dive more comfortable.

In waters having a temperature below 70° F., an exposure suit is definitely required. You will need a wet suit of at least ³⁄₁₆-inch thickness.

If you intend to dive in colder water—60° F. or less—you will need a full wet suit of ¼-inch thickness.

In 50° waters, you may need even more insulation, possibly wearing a ⅛-inch foam shirt or short suit under your full ¼-inch suit.

Exposure suits require proper maintenance. Rinse them in fresh water after immersion in salt water or in the heavily treated water found in most swimming pools. Sunlight and oil are the common causes of rapid deterioration of all rubber goods; exposure suits are no exception. Do not lubricate zippers or other parts of an exposure suit with petroleum oils or greases. Use a silicone lubricant instead.

WEIGHT BELTS

Dry suits and wet suits float. Adjust your buoyancy by adding or subtracting lead weights on a belt. Correct weight-

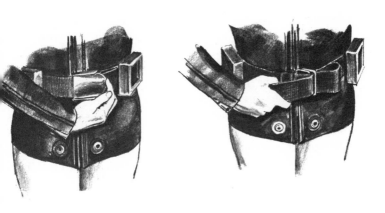

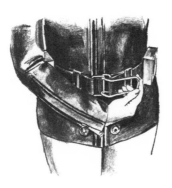

Figure 37. Quick releases.

ing is very important. If a diver is too heavily weighted, he will struggle to reach the surface. If he is too light, he will struggle to get below. Carry just enough weight so that you rise when you inhale and sink when you exhale. This is neutral buoyancy. Try this while floating on your back in shallow, protected water. Wear all the equipment you will be diving with, and be sure no air is trapped in your vest. Later you will see that neutral buoyancy at the surface will result in negative buoyancy at depth, since the increased water pressure will compress your exposure suit. If you have determined your ballast in fresh water but plan to dive in salt water, weigh yourself along with your full gear and your fresh-water ballast. Add 2½ percent of this total weight to your weight belt when you dive in salt water.

Your weight belt must be fastened only with a quick release. You must be able to jettison your weight belt almost instantly in an emergency. Any fastening that can be undone quickly with one hand in a single motion qualifies as a quick release. Some examples are illustrated. (See Figure 37.) You must also be able to jettison your partner's belt.

OPEN–WATER CONDITIONS

The forces which move the water in oceans, rivers and lakes can be enormous. These forces cannot be resisted by the diver. He must learn to work with them, even using them to his advantage. Currents generally run parallel to shore (littoral currents) or away from it at some angle (offshore currents). If you are caught in a current, let yourself drift for a few seconds to determine its direction, then swim shoreward at an angle to the current. If you try to swim directly against the flow, you will not make it. A rip current is a dangerous offshore current occurring off some beaches if surf is present. Look for a line of gaps in the breakers, marking the deep-water channel. Avoid this area.

92

Strong local currents may also be caused by the ebb and flow of the tide. The movement of vast quantities of water into and out of an area, as the tide rises or falls, may be channeled by valleys in the bottom, creating noticeable currents. Tidal-current tables (available from the U.S. National Ocean Survey) will tell you the direction and daily times of occurrence of important tidal currents in U.S. coastal areas. Familiarize yourself with the currents in your own area.

It is often possible to determine the existence, strength and direction of surface currents before you commit yourself and your partner to the water. Float a buoyant object in the water. If it moves appreciably, there is a current. Pick a diving area that has no major currents.

When diving from a boat, leave at least one person aboard who knows how to operate her. If your boat is unmanned and far from shore and you are carried away from her by a strong current, you are definitely in trouble. Inflate your vest and conserve your energy.

Bad weather will make diving conditions dangerous and unenjoyable. High surf and swell can produce seasickness as the diver tries to rest at the surface. A fog can make it difficult or impossible to find the beach or dive boat. Storms and fog are best avoided by checking the weather report before departing for the dive area.

The height of waves and surf is easily underestimated as you watch the sea from shore. Stand up or stoop as necessary to cause a distant wave crest to obscure the horizon slightly. The height of your eye above the water at the shoreline will then roughly equal the height of the distant wave. If you have to stand at your full height to align the wave crest with the horizon, the wave is at least as tall as you are. If you have to move a considerable distance up the slope of the beach, the wave is taller than you are. Do not attempt a dive in waves higher than a few feet.

93

DIVE PATTERNS

Open-water diving is always done in groups of two or more. Diving partners should stay in visual contact with each other. In-water visibility will dictate how close partners must be to maintain visual contact. In tropical waters, where 100-foot visibility is not uncommon, partners can swim much further apart than they can in northern waters, where 50-foot visibility might be considered excellent. In any case, stay close enough so that you can reach your partner quickly —in seconds—in an emergency.

An innertube float with a "divers down" flag attached is always towed by one member of the dive group. The flag is red with a diagonal white stripe, and serves to warn boats that divers are operating in the area. (See Figure 38.) Dives should not, however, be attempted in waters heavily traveled by boats. The float should comfortably support the entire group at the surface. If the float seems overloaded, the group is too large and should be subdivided into two or more separate groups, each having its own float and flag. The float provides an immediately available support for resting, adjusting gear or just talking. Tow the float with a line. Wrap the end of the line around your hand, but do not tie it to yourself. Keep yourself and your partners upstream of the line. Tangles can be serious, so you should carry a knife.

The float also provides a point of reassembly in case members of the group become separated. Agree before starting the dive that loss of contact among any of the divers will be a signal for the entire group to surface immediately at the float. Hopefully the missing divers will show up there. If they do not, the group can take the necessary search action.

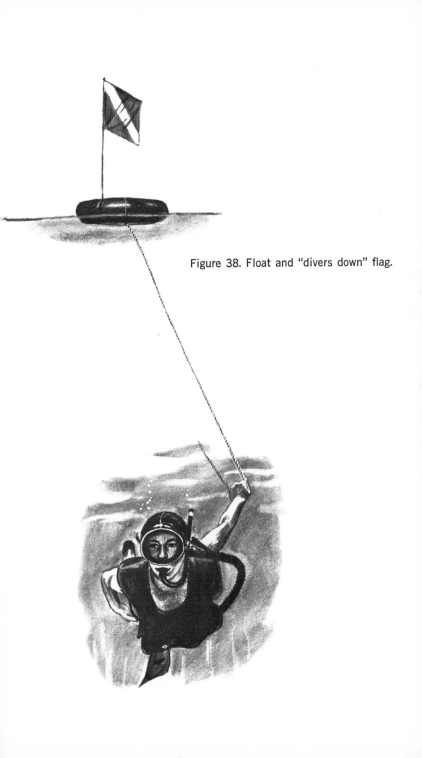

Figure 38. Float and "divers down" flag.

JUST A BEGINNING

Once a diver, you will never again think of water in the old way. Your perspective will be transformed. You will discover that the water surface is not a barrier or an ending, but a beginning. The joys of experiencing the open water start as you submerge.